AUSTRALIAN WILDERNESS

Captions Fleur Robertson **Design** Judith Chart
Commissioning Editor Andrew Preston **Editorial** Jane Adams and Gill Waugh
Production Ruth Arthur, David Proffit and Sally Connolly **Director of Production** Gerald Hughes
Director of Publishing David Gibbon

CLB 2554
© 1990 Colour Library Books Ltd, Godalming, Surrey, England
All rights reserved
Colour separations by Hong Kong Graphic Arts, Hong Kong
Printed and bound by Leefung Asco Printers Ltd, Hong Kong
ISBN 0 86283 813 4

AUSTRALIAN WILDERNESS

COOMBE

Australia is an enormous land. Here, a man can stand and look from one horizon to another, from one year's end to another and never see another human being. The vast reaches of arid land in the outback may see a plume of dust kicked up as a vehicle travels the long, lonely miles between stations. Or the bush may echo to the roar of a chain saw. But the endless horizons are largely untouched by civilization and industry. There are vast stretches of outback and bush where no white man has trodden to this very day, but the Aborigines have been there.

According to the original inhabitants of this continent, the land had its origins in the magical Dreamtime: a time when Nurunderi strode the land in search of his wives; a time when the sticks of the sky people burst into flame and created the sun. During this time of gods, animal spirits and fabulous ancestors the world was created amid violent passions and quarrels.

The white man, a newcomer to these shores, has a more prosaic, but probably more accurate, account of the formation of the continent. As the molten surface of the primeval planet cooled, it formed the great chunks of rock that are today's continents. Australia was one of these. It seems that, some 200 million years ago, Australia was linked with the other continents of the southern hemisphere in the supercontinent of Gondwanaland. But some time during the 'Age of the Dinosaurs', the Mesozoic era, Gondwanaland broke up and Australia drifted away into the quiet isolation that was to last for millions of years.

It is often said that Australia is the world's oldest continent. This is obviously not true, for all the continents were formed at about the same time, some 4,000,000,000 years ago. What is true, however, is that Australia contains some of the oldest rocks in the world, some 3,000,000,000 years old, which outcrop in Western Australia. The continent has remained, geologically, remarkably stable and peaceful for an immense period of time. The titanic forces that raised the Rocky Mountains and the Alps, indeed all the major mountains of the world, passed Australia by. The most recent Australian mountains were thrown up in the late Palaeozoic era, long before even the dinosaurs walked the earth. The weathered stumps of these mountains form the Great Dividing Range of the present day. The immense length of time during which little has happened has made Australia a land of low relief and few mountains. Only some six per cent of the land is over 2,000 feet in altitude and the maximum height of 7,316 feet is dwarfed by that of all the other continents.

With such a long history of geological stability behind it, it is perhaps natural that the landscape of the great continent has remained largely unaltered since the time when the first European arrived on the land. Though the settlers have brought industry to the land and settlements have sprung up across the country, the irresistible forces of nature have forbidden the interior to civilization and have given it a somewhat tenuous grip on the bush.

On Ash Wednesday, 1983, the citizens of Victoria were made painfully aware of the powerful forces of nature. For millions of years the plant life of Australia had been evolving and adapting to fit the environment. The gum tree forests that covered much of the southeast of the continent are ideally suited to the hot, dry climate. But when the European settlers arrived they brought European trees with them. Oaks and elms proliferated across the land and in many instances even supplanted the local, indigenous gums. On that Wednesday, however, the slenderness of their hold was revealed. A long, hot spell was followed by the scent of smoke from the north. Soon the whole countryside was a blazing inferno as the tinder-dry forests took light, fanned by a strong, hot wind. Villages and towns were devastated and the imported trees decimated, but the native gums had endured eons of bushfires and soon burst into bud again.

In a country that covers some seven and a half million square kilometres, but has a population of just thirteen million, there are bound to be areas where the landscape is just as nature formed it. And what a marvellously diverse landscape it is.

The mountainous island state of Tasmania stands like a sentinel in the raging seas south of the mainland. The attraction of the land lies in its diversity and character. The rich orchards of the historic Huon Valley make a pleasant contrast to the wilds of the mountains and west coast. Here, the dreaded horizontal – a small, densely growing tree – bars any exploration from the ground by even the most experienced bushwhacker. It is in these hidden lands that the Tasmanian wolf is thought still to survive, far away from the intrusions of man. The jagged peaks of the mountains tower majestically above the lakes that are such a feature of the central plateau region. The great eucalyptus forests and scrubland make up a unique area of great natural beauty where marsupials and native birds flourish.

Across the Bass Strait lies the state of Victoria, which has been aptly named the Garden State for, despite the fires, it is one of the most fertile and pleasant regions in the nation. Reaching up to the skies are the smooth ridges of the Southern Alps. In the winter the snow-covered peaks form a fairyland of glistening snow and ice, where crystal icicles hang from the branches. The foothills of these mountains are rolling, scenic landscapes; a wonderland at any time of the year.

As well as some of the densest forest on the continent, Victoria contains vast areas of mallee. This open eucalyptus scrubland once covered far more land, since much has been cleared and is now farmed for grain. The mallee may not be as scenically beautiful as the mountains, but it is fascinating nonetheless. The wildlife that scurries around in the undergrowth includes wallabies, roos and emus, and the unique mallee fowl.

The mighty Murray River flows westwards across the landscape, bringing life-giving moisture to the land. Beyond the tumbling waters of Australia's greatest river, beyond the rich orchards and farmlands of Riverina, beyond the black stump itself, stretch the wide pastoral lands that are the basis of the nation's animal wealth. The seemingly endless grasslands stretch away to the horizon in all directions. The lonely visitor is left with a feeling of his own insignificance set against the sheer scale of nature's vastness. The verdant landscape is broken only by sheep and by the station worker mustering his charges for shearing. Some seventy million sheep are sheared in the area annually, but even they can seem lost in this vast land.

The great tracts of grazing land reach eastwards to the foothills of the Great Dividing Range and westwards to the edge of the great deserts. Northwards, the land runs on across the Darling Downs, west of Brisbane, into the hot, tropical land of Queensland. On the other side of the Great Dividing Range the landscape is one of fertile ground and luxurious, sandy beaches until the dramatic Glasshouse Mountains are reached. These sheer plugs of volcanic rock that rise so suddenly from the plains are the remains of the violent eruptions that shook the region millions of years ago. The central vents of the volcanoes became clogged with molten magma which then solidified. As the surrounding cone eroded, the vertical plug was left standing free.

Along the northeast coast of the continent, east of the Great Dividing Range, lie stretches of steamy tropical rainforest. The lush greenery of the rainforest is dependent upon the regular dousing that comes with each tremendous downpour. In such a humid climate the rate of growth of the plants is phenomenal. In the race to survive, many plants use ingenious and sinister methods. The pitcher plants lure insects to the edge of the pitcher by exuding nectar, then trap and digest them in a secreted enzyme. The strangling fig grows around the trunk of a host tree, eventually destroying it.

Off the sultry coast lies one of nature's wonders: the Great Barrier Reef. A tropical wonderland of colourful fish and rich sealife is based upon the coral reef itself, which lies some miles offshore. The reef is composed of the remains of thousands of generations of tiny animals, but it is its size that is so staggering. For more than 2,000 kilometres the crashing surf of the Pacific Ocean throws its spray high into the air over the jagged points of the reef. The coral reaches the surface, where it is bathed in the strong sunlight, and in places plunges as deep as seventy metres into the dark depths to the sea floor. In and out of the cracks and crevices of the coral formations swim and crawl starfish, lobsters, angel fish, turtles and a whole host of other strange and exotic species. Across the 207,000 square kilometres of the reef's area there are many hundreds of idyllic tropical islands. Many of these have become popular resorts with Australians as they chase the sun.

Cape York is difficult to travel through and, indeed, for the average traveller it is all but impossible. The combination of steep escarpments, plunging chasms and broad rivers, not to mention the almost complete lack of roads, put the area beyond the reach of all but the most determined and experienced. The impenetrable, swampy jungles of northern Cape York make a fitting end to one of the wildest and most beautiful regions of the country. The vast area of land north of Mossman is populated only by the inhabitants of a few mining settlements and by Aboriginal communities. This is surely one of the last great, untamed wildernesses left on earth.

During the dry season the few roads and tracks of the area make for exciting four-wheel motoring. But during the 'Big Wet' the few roads and many fords become completely impassable as untamed nature takes over and undoes the work of man. To the southwest the murky mangrove swamps around the Gulf of Carpentaria have always defied the attempts of man to explore their interior. The sticky, shifting mud and close-growing stems and roots have made the area inaccessible to civilization.

In contrast, the great stretches of the Channel Country to the south are forbidding because of their very dryness. In this land of endless horizons the dust disturbed by the traveller's boots is the only moving thing visible amid the scrub and dirt. But the flat, arid lands undergo a startling change when the waters come. It does not actually rain in the Channel Country. The water pours down the Cooper, Georgina and Hamilton rivers as the clouds burst far to the north. Millions of gallons of water tumble across the arid plains, rushing south in their attempt to reach Lake Eyre. But the desert heat and water holes account for every drop of moisture before it can reach the great salt lakes. Thanks to the water there is a sudden profusion of greenery and floral splendour that makes the desert seem a veritable paradise. Animals, both wild and domestic, come in their thousands to feed on the lush pasture before the sun withers it into dust again.

Despite the terrible heat and burning sun of the interior, the waters that gush across the sands do sometimes actually reach the great salt lakes – occasionally, a trickle of water will run into the lake beds and moisten them. In 1950, and again in 1989, however, the rains that fell far to the north were nothing short of tremendous. Raging floods gushed across the Channel Country and several thousand square kilometres of Lake Eyre were under water. The influx of water dissolved the millions of tonnes of salt and the vast area of water became as salty as the sea. In 1950, fish appeared and survived for some time before the water evaporated in the scorching heat and the lake reverted to its normal, desolate self. Another of the empty lakes, Lake Yamma Yamma, is remarkable for its flat shores. When it has water in it, a steady wind can shift the position of the lake considerably.

South of Lake Eyre is the town of Maree, the start of the Birdsville Track. This famous stock track winds across the interior to Birdsville in Queensland and was once an important trade route. West of Maree, beyond Woomera, stretch the great expanses of the Nullarbor. This mighty, 260,000 square kilometre desert is underlain by a plateau of limestone, which accounts, in part, for its appearance and its name. The underlying rock is remarkably flat and it is this that gives the unique, endless flatness to the area, while the thin soil that it has produced accounts for the vegetation. Unable to hold moisture or to accommodate deep roots, the soil has imposed a herbaceous growth on the land. No tree, nor even a large shrub, can gain a foothold and only small plants with shallow root systems manage to survive. This has given the desert its name, which derives from *nullus arbor*, the Latin for 'no tree'.

For many years this great expanse of burning, shadeless waste was an almost unassailable block to communications. Today, however, there is both a road and a rail link across the 'no-tree' desert. The railway includes the longest stretch of straight track in the world; some 483 kilometres of it. Between Eucla and Bookabie the Eyre Highway runs close to the Cliffs of the Nullarbor, where the limestone plateau plunges from a dizzying height to the crashing surf of the Great Australian Bight. It was in this stretch of sea that Matthew Flinders lost his anchors in 1803.

Across the Nullarbor and beyond the gold-rich desert towns of Kalgoorlie and Coolgardie is the fertile southwest around Perth and Albany. Vast areas of the region have been given over to cereal growing. Between Geraldton and Albany is a great sweep of golden grain fields, waving in the sparkling sunlight as the soft breeze stirs the corn. Some two million hectares of Western Australia's best land are given over to crop production, while much of the rest is pasture.

For thousands of years, this fertile area has been separated to the north and east from the rest of the island continent by great stretches of desert. Being isolated from a continent that was itself isolated from the rest of the world has had a profound effect on the flora of the region. The rugged mountains of the Stirling Range and Porongurups rise above majestic stands of karri and tingle. The tree trunks rise sheer, like smooth pillars, to the canopy far above and some giants may reach a height of fully sixty metres. But it is the less dramatic plants that are the more impressive by dint of their sheer beauty and numbers.

In the spring, vast areas of land become carpeted with shades of colour of every description as millions upon millions of flowers burst their buds. There are some three thousand species of wild flowers in the area south of the Murchison River and the vast majority of them are found nowhere else on earth: a legacy of the region's isolation. The arresting scarlet of the bottlebrushes shines out from the depths of the bush as the delicate blooms bob in the breeze. The yellow or red banksias hold their bright cylinders high to the sun, the flowers seeming so alien to the drab shrub that produces them. Further north, as the land becomes more arid, the ephemerals take over the landscape. Brought to life by the infrequent showers of the region, mulla mullas and everlastings erupt from the bare soil and carpet it with a sea of colour. Of all these desert ephemerals, perhaps the best known and most colourful is Sturt's Desert Pea, whose scarlet and black blooms can be found right across the continent's arid interior.

The land further north may be less inviting, but its scenic beauty increases to the truly spectacular. Standing on the sandy desert floor like soldiers on parade are the Pinnacles: a bizarre, almost unearthly formation created by the trunks of long-petrified trees being exposed amid the sand.

Beyond the Gascoyne River, which actually flows a few feet beneath the river bed, stretch the Pilbara and the Hammersley Range. Intermittent streams, often only metres wide, have carved plunging canyons from the richly coloured rock. The walls of the chasms, which may tower as high as a hundred metres, are made up of myriad hues that darken or glow in the sunlight. Dales Gorge is over forty-five kilometres long and contains the magnificent Fortescue Falls. The streams that have cut such glorious features into the earth only flow when there has been rain, but along their courses billabongs hold the water throughout the year. At Millstream, thousands of birds swoop down to drink the thirst-quenching water that is the clearest for miles and, in so doing, make a magnificent show amid the rushes and ferns.

The Kimberley region lies in the north, bordering the Timor Sea, and is an area of rugged beauty and scenery. Near Halls Creek are situated two natural curiosities. The first is a crater some 850 metres across and sixty metres deep, marking the spot where a massive meteorite smashed into the earth a million years ago. The second is a white stone wall that looks man-made. In fact, it is a vertical seam of quartz that has eroded more slowly than the surrounding soft rock and has been left standing free.

The coast around Arnhem Land is one of dense mangrove swamps and thick, sticky mud. Behind the impenetrable mass of mangroves lies a forest of distinctly tropical, almost Malaysian, character. The weather is uncomfortably warm and wet for most of the year, and an annual rainfall of over two metres is not unusual. Further south the climate becomes progressively drier as the effects of the monsoon peter out. The forests and crocodile-infested rivers first give way to open forest land and then to the valuable pastureland of the Barkly Tableland.

But it is far to the south that the heart and focus of the great, untamed Australian outback is to be found: the Red Centre.

Vast seas of shifting red sands march across the landscape for hundreds of miles in dunes up to forty metres high. The great Simpson Desert covers 145,000 square kilometres of the Centre and swallows up the Todd and Hay rivers in its burning, arid depths. The symmetrical ridges of the great MacDonnell Ranges run to the horizons and are cut by majestic chasms. Here the dancing sunlight plays on the water surface and scatters in myriad bouncing lights on the burning red walls of the canyons. Strange and wonderful rock formations shelter the weird wildlife that scampers around in the shadows, including lizards with fearsome frills and reptiles with spikes like some nightmare monster.

All this grandeur, magnificence and desolation revolves around one spot. At the heart of the Red Centre, at the heart of the continent, stands the gigantic Ayers Rock. Rising above the flat, featureless landscape like a monstrous behemoth, the Rock surveys the creation around it. In its untamed bulk, it signifies the wildness and beauty that is Australia.

Previous page: a rock formation known as the Loop, in Kalbarri National Park, where the Murchison River has carved a spectacular gorge, a colourful stretch of canyon that is chiefly responsible for the popularity of the park.

Above: scorched terrain around Wittenoom, where the red earth, golden dry grass and startling blue skies combine to form a landscape both harsh and beautiful.

Right: the dark blue waters of Dales Gorge, in Hammersley Range National Park, the state's second largest national reserve. Deprived of the sun for most of the day, such pools of water can be startlingly cold.

Facing page: a maroon coloured cliff face in Rio Tinto Gorge in the northern section of Hammersley Range National Park, where millions of years of geological pressure have created incredible rock formations.

Above: Fortescue Falls cascade down steps of richly coloured strata in Hammersley Range National Park's Dale Gorge, where red rock is embroidered by creams, grey and golds.

Left: glowing like a red-hot coal in the light of evening, a rock face in the Hammersley Range is typical of this national park's mineral-rich terrain. It comes as no surprise to learn that iron ore is particularly plentiful here – these are virtually mountains of iron.

These pages: electric light reveals the beauty of stalactites that formerly hung in darkness in the depths of Jewel Cave, part of Cape Leeuwin-Naturaliste National Park on the Western Australian seaboard. Situated near Augusta, this is a limestone cave full of fragile stalactites, and stalagmites over thirty feet in circumference. Pools of still water decorate the caves and, untouched by any breeze, perfectly reflect the sharp-toothed formations.

Storm-carved rocks on the beach at Broome, sometimes called the Port of Pearls, a town that was the centre of a thriving pearling industry during the last century, when Japanese, Filipino and Indonesian immigrants worked offshore pearl grounds. The shore itself bears evidence of much earlier visitors; at the foot of sandstone cliffs close to Broome lie the fossil footprints of a prehistoric creature, which are believed to be 150 million years old.

Above: red and gold rock, carved by wind and water, fills Kalbarri National Park, which lies some 150 kilometres north of Geraldton and is famous for its coloured cliffs. The most interesting of these are to be found alongside the Murchison River, which flows through a region of primeval beauty.

Facing page: Murchison River Gorge, Kalbarri National Park. The park, which covers 186,000 hectares, encompasses the lower reaches of this river until it meets the Indian Ocean at Red Bluff. It also contains numerous, quite magnificent flowering trees.

The peculiar rock formations known as the Pinnacles in the Pinnacles Desert of Nambung National Park. Each standing in a saucer of sand, these lumps of limestone range in size from stony footballs to pillars more than six metres tall. Not far from this field of eerie rocks are unusual white sand drifts, another feature of Nambung. The park, which lies 200 kilometres north of Perth on the southwest coast, consists of terrain so severe that those who wish to explore the area are obliged to use four-wheel-drive vehicles.

These pages: Pinnacles Desert in Nambung National Park, where the power of the wind to erode solid rock is evident – these spikes of limestone owe their shape to the ability of the prevailing winds to blast minute amounts of sand against them, thereby grinding them slowly away.

These pages: stark, leafless branches reach out to the horizon along the coastline between Cape Leeuwin and Cape Naturaliste in the southwest of the state. Much of this shoreline, a distance of some one hundred miles, lies within Cape Leeuwin-Naturaliste National Park, a series of reserves noteworthy for their limestone caves – there are over 120 of them here. From Cape Leeuwin, which lies on the southwest tip of Australia, one can see the sun rise over one ocean and set over another.

Above: 'Natural Bridge' rock formation on the state's southern coast in Torndirrup National Park, which is especially famous for its romantic, rugged shoreline and the roaring waves of the great Southern Ocean.

Right: white horse waves thunder onto the rocks at Cape Leeuwin, where the confluence of two oceans – the Indian and the Southern – ensures that the seas are often wild. For a place of such fierce weather, the name of the cape is apt. Leeuwin, which means lioness in Dutch, was the name of the Dutch ship that was the first to reach these waters in 1622.

Superb surf curls to the shore in Torndirrup National Park, which lies southwest of the town of Albany, the first town to be established in Western Australia. In 1826, Major Edmund Lockyer landed here to claim the western half of the continent as British territory.

Left: children 'ride the wave' at Wave Rock, a geological phenomenon lying east of Hyden in Western Australia's Central Hinterland. Stretching for several hundred yards, this fifteen-metre-high eroded outcrop is estimated to be 2,700 million years old.

Above: wind-sculpted rock, aptly named Hippo's Yawn, dwarfs visitors. Situated close to Wave Rock, this louring piece of granite was also formed by the wind. Both features have been coloured in vertical bands by rain, which washes chemical deposits out of the stone and down the rock faces.

Above: the subtle hues of a water lily lit by the sun against the dark waters of Fogg Dam, near the town of Humpty Doo, seventy kilometres southeast of Darwin in the north of the territory.

Right: a cormorant prepares to roost as evening turns to night at Fogg Dam. The dam was constructed in the 1950s to provide water for the irrigation of potentially fertile soil at the 'Top End' and facilitate the production of crops such as rice.

These pages: Fogg Dam Bird Sanctuary, which is home to huge flocks of waterbirds, particularly pelicans and elegant, white egrets, though galahs, cockatoos and kitehawks can also be seen. In this tropical climate, animal and plant life thrives. Many of the animals, such as crocodiles and wallabies, can be observed at sunrise or sunset as they move between their feeding grounds and their sleeping areas.

Above and top: freshwater crocodiles, which can grow up to several metres in length. Despite the fact that the Northern Territories have three rivers named 'alligator', there are no alligators in Australia. Early settlers mistook one for the other when they christened these waterways.

Right: the East Alligator River sweeps through Arnhem Land, a vast aboriginal reserve that occupies almost half of the Top End and to which entry is strictly controlled. As it reaches the sea, the East Alligator River forms part of the border between Arnhem Land and Kakadu National Park.

These pages: long shadows in Stanley Chasm, where, at the end of the day, the lack of light turns the sides of this famous cleft in the MacDonnell Ranges to a dark brown. At noon, however, the walls blaze with colour as sunlight turns these sheer rockfaces to burning reds and golds. These are set against creamy gold sands on the chasm floor that seem white in the brilliant light of midday.

An abandoned opencast iron ore mine. Only comparatively recently – in the last few decades – has mining started to challenge cattle rearing as one of the territory's primary industries. The mining of iron ore is centred upon Mount Bundey and Frances Creek near Darwin, but other minerals are widespread – the Northern Territory has been among the country's most important copper- and gold-producing regions for the past twenty years.

These pages: Palm Valley Flora and Fauna Reserve, which lies west of Alice Springs in the MacDonnell Ranges. The reserve takes its name from the *Livistona mariae* palms, which, totally unique to this valley, are much in evidence in the long, twisting gorge of the Finke River that forms its centrepiece. The valley was discovered in 1872 by the explorer Ernest Giles.

Over 1,000 metres high in places, the thirty peaks of the Olgas are held sacred by the Yankuntjatjara and Pitjandjara Aboriginal tribes of the area around Alice Springs and feature significantly in their ritual life and myths.

These pages: the Olgas, one of the rock massifs that form part of Uluru National Park, a region now deeded to the Aborigines and leased by them back to the nation. These rock massifs, whose highest peak, Mount Olga, was named for a nineteenth-century queen of Spain, are a range of mountains over seven kilometres in length.

Against an evening sky falling from indigo to ice blue, the Olgas glow rust red, black shadows distinguishing their clefts and crevices. The tribes of the region called the range 'Kata Tjuta', meaning 'mountain of many heads', and indeed, although there are many seemingly separate domes in the range, this sandstone massif is one entity under the desert, buried up to its 'neck'.

These pages: Ayers Rock. Subtly changing colour
throughout the day and burning blood red at sunset, the
monolith Uluru, as the Aborigines call Ayers Rock,
seems to command the entire 'Red Centre' in its majesty.

Rising abruptly out of the featureless plain of scrub and sand that forms Uluru National Park, Ayers Rock stands as the continent's most unforgettable natural image. Deposited 600 million years ago during the Cambrian period, the monolith, like the Olgas, is buried up to its 'neck' in sand, only the summit of a mighty mountain being visible today.

Moon-like in its pockmarked surfaces, Ayers Rock is 348 metres high and extremely arduous to ascend. Ominous warnings are posted at its foot, alerting the casual climber to the dangers of attempting the summit without adequate preparation and a certain degree of fitness, both physical and mental.

The extensive reserve known as Carnarvon National Park, which lies some 700 kilometres northwest of Brisbane in south Queensland. This reserve is dissected by Carnarvon Creek, whose course can easily be charted across the Great Dividing Range since it has scored a magnificent, 600-foot-deep gorge through the sandstone. High cliffs and palms are features of the park, as are a variety of caves containing Aboriginal rock carvings.

Facing page: the sheer, jagged rock face that edges
Carnarvon Creek, the centrepiece of Carnarvon National
Park. In time, this rock too will break and be rounded
into pebbles by the creek's swift and powerful current.
Carnarvon Creek has numerous tributaries where dark,
deep pools are still the haunt of the duck-billed
platypus. In places, these side gorges can be 200-feet
deep, yet only six feet in width.

Above: part of a moss garden in Carnarvon National
Park. The wild flowers that bloom in this reserve in
early spring are one of the highlights of the region.

Above: maidenhair ferns and a variety of mosses thrive amid constantly dripping water in Carnarvon National Park.

Facing page: beautiful Cedar Creek creates a watery aisle between soaring trees in one of the ten Tamborine Mountain Parks, which lie close to the state's Gold Coast.

Malanda Falls, one of numerous waterfalls in Atherton Tableland, a fascinating plateau that lies approximately fifty kilometres from Cairns. This region was named for John Atherton, a pioneer farmer who established a farm on the plateau in 1877. Today the Tableland holds seven national parks, but it wasn't until discoveries of tin and gold were made under a hundred years ago that large numbers of white men started to settle here.

Although the dark shadows of twilight hide a heron from view, its distinctive reflection reveals its presence on the banks of Fairbairn Reservoir south of Emerald in Queensland's Central Highlands. Despite its name, Emerald began as a mining town centred upon copper and gold. Today its inhabitants use the reservoir for leisure and water sports.

Facing page: mounts Beerwah and Coonowrin, two of ten eroded volcanic plugs that comprise the Glasshouse Mountains, a range on the state's southern coast which was discovered and named by Captain Cook in 1770.

Above: Maroon Dam, south of Boonah near the New South Wales border, its smooth lawns giving it the air of a vast landscaped garden belonging to a country estate.

Left: Nixon Creek, sun-dappled and swift, finds a route through the rainforest in Lamington National Park, Queensland's most popular reserve. Lamington contains over 700 species of orchids of every size and colour, it boasts a senses nature trail, designed for the blind and its challenging rockfaces are favoured by climbers.

Above: a sluggish river carves the head of a snake from the rainforest of tropical north Queensland.

Right: the leaves of sugar cane are destroyed in a flash fire lit for the purpose prior to harvesting. Only the stalks of cane remain after the flames have subsided, making the process of cutting and collecting them cleaner and quicker.

Facing page: a field of young sugar cane stretches to the foothills in northern Queensland. In the last century it was alleged that the sugar industry would collapse if plantation owners were deprived of their cheap *kanaka* labour from the Pacific islands, but, though legislation did ultimately cut off this source, the industry survived – and prospered – through mechanisation. Today Queensland produces ninety-five per cent of the nation's sugar.

Above: the north Queensland coast near Cairns, spread with rainforest. The waters of the Coral Sea here are justifiably considered some of the finest in the southern hemisphere.

Facing page: flanked by shallows of fine, white sand, a river curves at the foot of jungle-clad hills in north Queensland. This state is not only extremely fertile, capable of producing grain, cotton, peanuts and timber, and raising cattle and sheep, it also contains enormous quantities of minerals, such as copper, lead and zinc.

Ringed by surf, edged with sand and surrounded by blue sea for as far as the eye can see, a serene and lush islet of the Great Barrier Reef epitomises the popular vision of a faraway desert island.

These pages: cays of the Great Barrier Reef, the spectacle of which alone is worth a visit to Australia. At over 2,000 kilometres in length – stretching from the coast of western Papua to the coast of Queensland – this coral reef is the longest in the world, and the most wonderful. Amid a staggering array of multi-coloured coral gardens swim shoals of shining fish, each a sprinkling of gemstones against the backcloth of these warm blue waters.

As the world's largest coral formation, the Great Barrier Reef is a living phenomenon. Its coloured coral branches sit upon banks of limestone polyps which have accumulated over thousands of years. These banks are separated by channels of water, which, according to their depth, are shaded from the most delicate greens to the darkest blues.

Veined rocks flank a fine beach in Korora Bay, north of Coffs Harbour. Apart from its attractive beach, Korora can also boast the Bruxner Park Flora Reserve, a dense tropical jungle area of vines, ferns and orchids that offers bushwalking tracks and a picnic area.

Above: a beachcomber's four-wheel-drive on the shore at Coffs Harbour emphasizes the lonely beauty of this coastline when deserted by its sizeable quota of sun-lovers. Coffs Harbour is a popular holiday resort for Sydneysiders – for many, lying on such a superb stretch of sand is still 'the most Australian thing you can do' (Ross Terrill).

Facing page: surf rolls in over a Port Macquarie beach, which is exceptionally good for fishing, especially when the bream run in winter. Another holiday destination, the town is one of the oldest in New South Wales; it was founded in 1821 and, like many communities along Australia's Pacific coast, grew up as a convict settlement.

A lone rowing boat, its colour camouflaging it against the pale cream sand, lies out of reach of the tide on Shelley Beach. Situated on the outskirts of Port Macquarie, this beach is one of the area's best loved beauty spots, and as such has long been favoured by Australian and overseas painters.

Facing page: a creek becomes a heavy veil of white
water at Ellenborough Falls on the Comboyne Plateau, a
day's drive from Port Macquarie. These falls, which drop
150 metres, are one of many dazzling cascades hidden
in a largely inaccessible wilderness of dense forest near
the township of Comboyne.

Above: a multitude of tropical plants in Rainforest Gully,
part of the lush National Botanic Gardens on the lower
slopes of Black Mountain in Canberra. The gardens,
which are devoted to plants and trees native to
Australia, consist of specialised areas of vegetation
indigenous to various Australian regions.

Above: the imposing outcrop of rock pinnacles known as the Three Sisters at Echo Point near the township of Katoomba in Blue Mountains National Park. The Blue Mountains are easily travelled via a road that runs along the park's flat-topped ridges, but parts of the thickly forested valley floor are so difficult to cross that only skilled bushwalkers are advised to try.

Facing page: bright creams and golds in the jagged limestone walls of the Kanangra Plateau startle the eye against the seemingly endless soft folds and shadows of the Blue Mountains.

Facing page and above: Wentworth Falls, a latticework of flowing water and rock strata and one of the most breathtaking sights in Blue Mountains National Park. So thick and unspoilt is the vegetation here that the gorge seems almost prehistoric.

Left: the laughing kookaburra, which, although it is only found in Australia, is known throughout the world for its endearing, jovial chuckle. Heard mainly in the early morning and evening, often its laughing call is a communal affair, with the entire family or nesting group joining in.

Weeping Rock Falls in Blue Mountains National Park. The park is centred upon the Grose River Valley, which has cut 2,500 feet down through colourful sandstones, shales and coal measures to form a beautiful gorge. There are many waterfalls and fern glens within the 245,000 acres that comprise the reserve, and distinctive wild flowers are to be found in spring on the sandstone plateau heights. Situated forty miles west of Sydney, the park is one of the state's most popular.

Above: an aerial view of the arid terrain between White Cliffs and Broken Hill, where hardy vegetation follows the path of a dry riverbed and water is at a premium.

Right: unripe bananas on a plantation at Coffs Harbour, a coastal town based upon the banana-growing industry. The clusters of upturned fruits are called 'hands', the individual bananas being known as 'fingers'. At harvesting, the entire plant is cut down, since it bears fruit only once.

Facing page: milky water destined to evaporate forms a temporary pool amid scrubland around Broken Hill. Although this land is infertile and apparently worthless to man, it is rich in minerals – the town of Broken Hill is built on the largest silver-zinc-lead deposit in the world.

Above: red earth dehydrates to dust in far western New South Wales, where rainfall is sparse and reservoirs are essential to support livestock and people.

Right: ghost gums thrive in a virtually dry riverbed, their white trunks conspicuous against the ochre coloured sand, their leafy branches shielding the last pools of water from the sun. Occasionally, in such riverbeds one can see driftwood high in the branches of a tree, deposited there by a flash flood when sudden rain filled the waterway again.

Above: a black swan and cygnet push through floating leaves. The only swan native to Australia, the black swan has some white feathers but these are seldom seen when the bird is at rest, the white edges of the wings being most noticeable when it is in flight.

Right: one of the Menindee Lakes, designed to store water from the Darling River to supply the mining town of Broken Hill. The lakes cover 16,200 hectares and provide fine – if unexpected – opportunities for sailing enthusiasts.

These pages: the flooded forest. Saturated when the Darling River was diverted to store water, the stark trunks of dead trees, as well as thriving live ones, populate Lake Menindee in western New South Wales. It was at Menindee that the ill-fated Victorian explorers Burke and Wills stayed before the party divided, leaving nine men to push north to the Gulf of Carpentaria. In those days, Menindee was a frontier town and only unknown territory lay beyond it.

Whisky Bay, part of Wilson's Promontory National Park in southern Victoria, which is situated on the southernmost tip of the Australian mainland. This park, one of Victoria's largest and most popular, boasts an impressive number of varied landscapes, including tall forests, salt marshes and long drifts of sand dunes. There are more than eighty kilometres of walking tracks and the wildlife to be seen along them is often surprisingly tame.

These pages: the footprints of visitors await obliteration by the next high tide as dusk falls in Whisky Bay. Lying on the east of the peninsula that forms Wilson's Promontory National Park, this bay is typical of the glorious sand beaches to be found on 'The Prom', as it is locally known. Several such beaches are safe for swimming, especially near Norman Bay, while on one beach here – aptly named Squeaky Beach – the sand literally squeaks when trodden upon.

Above: Pyramid Rock, one of the distinctive tall rocks that form a group known as the Nobbies on Phillip Island, which lies at the entrance to Westernport Bay.

Right: hare's tail grass blows in the wind on a cliff top on Phillip Island.

Facing page: the Nobbies, the breeding ground for 5,000 fur seals at the southwest tip of Phillip Island. From the headland, it is possible to watch the seals with the use of a telescope.

These pages: Phillip Island, which is joined to the mainland via a narrow bridge at San Remo. The island's greatest attractions are its fairy penguins, who waddle back from the sea each evening, quite unperturbed by the rapt audience of humans that assembles to see them.

As the sun sinks behind a cloudy horizon, a lone tree is silhouetted in Stratford Highway Park, near Sale. Sale, which is built beside the Thompson River, is the main administrative city in Gippsland, an area that has grown rich since the exploitation of offshore oil reserves in Bass Strait – indeed, Sale itself achieved a certain boomtown status at the time of the discovery.

These pages: wild flowers on Mount William, the highest peak in a sandstone range of mountains in western Victoria known as the Grampians. In 1836 Mount William was climbed by one Major Mitchell, who went on to name these peaks after the Grampian range of his native Scotland. Apart from their scenic grandeur, these mountains are best known for the beauty and variety of their wild flowers. There are more than a thousand species of ferns and flowering plants native to the region, most of which are at their most colourful from August until November.

Above: the McKenzie Falls, on the McKenzie River in the Grampians near Halls Gap. This little community, which today is the focal point of the area, takes its name from a pioneer farmer who settled in the eastern Grampians in the early 1840s.

Facing page: the Kiewa River near Falls Creek near the start of its journey to meet the great Murray River, which lies some 120 kilometres downstream and forms the northern border between Victoria and New South Wales.

Facing page: a floating carpet of water lilies blooms in San Remo, the little fishing village that is the gate to Phillip Island.

Above: moss-covered tree roots and exuberant fans of ferns in Tarra Valley-Bulga National Park, which lies in the Gippsland region near Yarram. Here two of Australia's most fascinating creatures – the lyrebird and the duck-billed platypus – can be found, and the park is also renowned for it rare tree ferns, which grow in abundance in the rainforest.

Above: a flock of gulls passes by at Port Campbell National Park, one of Victoria's forty national parks. Port Campbell stretches approximately thirty miles along the coast south of Warrnambool, a thin stretch of land marked by fascinating cliff formations.

Right: the stark branches of a flooded tree interrupt the serenity of a salt pond near Manangatang, a small town some forty kilometres from the Victoria/New South Wales border in the northeast of the state.

White sand and lush vegetation are the hallmarks of the shoreline at Seaspray on Ninety Mile Beach in Gippsland, south Victoria. All along this stretch of coastline a thin strip of land separates the shore from a parallel series of six lakes, Wellington, King, Victoria, Tyers, Reeve and Coleman, which forms Australia's largest system of inland waterways. Since just to the north lie the foothills of the alpine high country, and two national parks – the Lakes and the Glenaladale – are close by, it is not surprising that this region is Victoria's most outstanding holiday area.

These pages: a stark and seemingly lifeless landscape of petrified wood flanks the sea at Cape Bridgewater, near Portland. Such fossils are formed by the process of petrification, during which the wood fibres are gradually replaced by a mineral, usually silica or chalcedony. This replacement occurs very slowly, molecule by molecule, allowing the original appearance and structure of the wood to be maintained. Cape Bridgewater, a volcanic headland, is the highest point on the Victoria coast, and contains a collection of blowholes, near the petrified forest along the cliff top, that are particularly exciting to watch and listen to in rough weather.

These pages: Island Archway rock formation in Port Campbell National Park. This park stretches along the south Victoria coast from Peterborough in the west to the western bank of the Gellibrand River at Princetown, and covers an area of 700 hectares. Primarily known for its impressive cliffs, which are the finest in the state, the park is also notable for its offshore breeding colonies of mutton birds.

Facing page: lashed by water on all sides, Razorback Rock defies the Southern Ocean in Port Campbell National Park, where aggregates of clay, sand and limestone have been sculpted by the waves into fascinating shapes.

Above: the Sentinels in Port Campbell National Park, which, like the famous 'Twelve Apostles' rock stacks nearby, appear to have resisted the eroding power of the waves for centuries. Nevertheless, these rocks will succumb eventually, each destined to be washed away by the water – indeed, they are already one step further towards obliteration than the coastline's arches, which have yet to lose their connecting 'roofs'.

Above: one of the Twelve Apostles stacks that tower
several hundred feet above the sea in Port Campbell
National Park. Here the volatile Southern Ocean meets
the high, flat coastal plains as they form vertical,
virtually unscalable cliffs. Such 'dry' land was almost
more dangerous than the sea to the many who were
shipwrecked here in the last century as, even should
they reach them alive, it was impossible to ascend these
cliffs to escape the force of the thundering waves.

Right: sunset at the Crags, a romantic spot – though a
potentially treacherous one for sailing – on the shoreline
between Port Fairy and Yambuck.

Spring brings drifts of low cloud and lambs to a
windswept pasture outside Ouse, northwest of Hobart.
Ouse is part of Tasmania's main pastoral district, the
Midlands area between Oatlands and Perth, which is
noted for its high-quality merino wool and stock-raising.
One of the first farming areas established on the island,
it is the part of Tasmania most reminiscent of England.

Although many Australians liken Tasmania to England, few Englishmen would consider familiar the distinctly tropical vegetation of Mount Field National Park, eighty kilometres south of Hobart. This park, one of the first to be founded on the island, is one of the most popular, providing, among other facilities, the only developed skiing area in southern Tasmania. Tasmania contains remarkably varied flora and fauna and, fully aware of the need to preserve this, the state has dedicated over six per cent of its land to national parks – a greater percentage than has any other state.

Tasman Arch, an unusual coastal formation on the Tasman Peninsula and the main attraction of Tasman Arch and Waterfall Bay State Reserve, which lies southeast of the capital, Hobart. Other rock formations on the peninsula protected by state reserves are the Devil's Kitchen, the Blowhole and the Tessellated Pavement. The narrow isthmus of Eaglehawk Neck that leads to the peninsula was once guarded by a line of vicious tethered hounds to prevent convicts held on the peninsula from escaping.

Above: clear water and wild flowers, features of the coastline near Mayfield, a small town north of Triabunna in the east of the state. Mayfield overlooks Great Oyster Bay, across which lies the Freycinet Peninsula and Schouten Island. The peninsula and the island form Freycinet National Park, which offers the nature lover a wealth of wildlife, especially at Moulting Lagoon, where the black swan breeds.

Facing page: the Devil's Kitchen on the Tasman Peninsula, where sheer cliffs appear as if some human hand – rather than the waves – had fashioned their slab-like sides.

The Gordon Dam and Lake Gordon, both of which were born of the hydro-electric scheme that dammed the Gordon River. The Tasmanian state government was opposed in its decision to construct the dam by conservationists, who argued that the famous white-quartz beach of Lake Pedder, next to Lake Gordon, would be lost under the floodwater created by the dam. The government won and the beach was lost, yet, but for this, the beauty of Lake Pedder is considered to be unspoilt by the rise in the water level.

Above: Tasmanian devils, whose fierceness is legendary. Found only on Tasmania now, although their fossil remains have been discovered on mainland Australia, these creatures are unique among marsupials in having large heads and forequarters and powerful jaws. The size of a cocker spaniel dog, the Tasmanian devil lives on medium-sized mammals and birds, eating the entire carcass – including the skin, bones and fur or feathers.

Right: an arid western Tasmanian landscape. Although this island covers a mere 68,000 square kilometres, its geography and climate are considerably more varied than such a size might suggest. While the west is rugged and grand, its coastline full of high cliffs and rocky shores, the central plateau is broken by high mountains and narrow river valleys, and to the east the countryside is gentle, fertile and undulating.

Water plunges in several stages down into deep, rainforest-filled gorges at Russell Falls in Mount Field National Park. As a consequence of their picturesque setting, these falls are the park's best known, though there are several others considered equally beautiful in Mount Field. Established as a national park in 1916, this area consists of glacial lakes such as Lake Dobson, which is found at 3,450 feet, impressive peaks such as Mount Field West, which is nearly 5,000 feet high, and glacier-carved valleys and cirques. Alpine vegetation is present on the heights, while temperate rainforest grows on the slopes.

Facing page: St Columba Falls, the centrepiece of St. Columba Falls State Reserve, which covers an area of 314 hectares near St Helens in northeast Tasmania. The reserve is renowned for its excellent silver bream fishing and its forested mountain valleys: a beautiful forest canopy encloses the walk to the base of the falls.

Above: shorn sheep safely graze in countryside near Springfield, a small town in the northeast of the island.

Softly falling rain brings a rainbow to pastures in the Barossa Valley, whose fertile appearance belies the fact that South Australia is the driest state in the driest continent in the world – in all its vast area, there is scarcely one permanently running stream. Nevertheless, the state can boast one of the finest valleys for grape cultivation in all Australia, since the Barossa Valley is irrigated by the North and South Para rivers. Situated to the north of Adelaide, this valley was settled during the early part of the last century by Lutherans, who brought wine-making skills with them from Germany. Their descendants are still there today, and the valley retains a distinctly Germanic atmosphere.

Above: flowers for as far as the eye can see near Port Wakefield.

Right: pasture lying fallow on the Yorke Peninsula. This peninsula, settled now as agricultural country, was initially developed following the discovery here of copper ore deposits. Today, the three little towns of Wallaroo, Moonta and Kadina, which were established while the mines were being worked, are collectively known as Little Cornwall, because so many of the miners who flocked to this area were from Cornwall in England. In the May of every odd-numbered year the descendants of these miners hold a Cornish festival known as Kernewek Lowender.

Left: a tangle of fallen eucalypts form the foreground to a landscape of soft whites and russets as autumn approaches in Willowie Forest Reserve. This reserve is situated in the Flinders Ranges, a rugged chain of mountains that stretches from mid state into the continent's central deserts.

Above: a pretty-faced wallaby, distinguished from other bush wallabies by its striking white cheek markings and long, slender tail. There is no major difference between kangaroos and wallabies other than their size. The latter are smaller and they tend to inhabit more densely vegetated country than do kangaroos.

An outback road, beyond Penong, a town on the Eyre Highway. This famous road stretches several thousand kilometres along the coast and across the dead-flat Nullarbor Plain to connect Adelaide with Perth in Western Australia. Prior to 1976, when it was bitumen sealed, the highway had the reputation of being one of Australia's worst, since it resembled a dirt track in summer and a quagmire in winter. Even now, travelling its length should not be undertaken casually, since the Plain consists of little but semi-desert and human habitation is rare.

Eddies of salt dry in searing sunshine in an outback saltpan beyond the town of Penong. Eighty per cent of salt production in South Australia is derived from solar evaporation and is centred upon the indented coastline of the Gulf St Vincent and Spencer Gulf – the total annual production here is 700,000 tonnes.

Facing page Wilpena Pound in the Flinders Ranges
National Park. The former's rather prosaic name refers to
the area's huge, basin-like formation, its rough and
jagged rim being an encircling mountain range, its base
a plateau covering about eighty square kilometres.
Pioneer farmers saw it as a natural enclosure for stock –
hence its name. To Aborigines it was Wilpena, the
'place of bent fingers', which aptly describes the
Pound's resemblance to a cupped hand.

Above: sheep scratch a living on the Eyre Peninsula.

Above: a koala and its baby, which is carried in a pouch for the first six months of its life, completing its education on its mother's back. Restricted to a diet of leaves from only a few species of eucalypts, the koala is potentially as vulnerable as the panda, but, unlike the latter, it breeds sufficiently well in captivity to ensure its survival.

Right: the Barossa Valley. Although its name is a corruption of the Spanish for Hill of Roses, all the valley has in common with Spain is the excellence of its wine. Justifiably, Barossa's vintners have gained a worldwide reputation.

These pages: the arid golds and purple of Wilpena Flat, Bunyeroo, in the central Flinders Ranges. Three species of kangaroo are found in the Flinders Ranges, as are a variety of reptiles, including the intriguingly named Flinders Range earless dragon. The wedge-tailed eagle may also be seen here, alongside kestrels and honeyeaters, grey butcher birds and rufous whistlers. The region is also famed for its Aboriginal rock paintings and rock incisions. The ranges were named after the great navigator, Matthew Flinders, who sighted them in 1802 during his explorations in H.M.S. *Investigator*.

A red dust road in Wilpena Pound.